Tempting

Teatime
TREATS

T5-CQA-837

KÖNEMANN

Traditional Favorites

What could be more pleasant and relaxing than a leisurely afternoon tea? Get out your best cups and saucers, set a pretty table and take the time to make some of these classic recipes, to give your guests a rare and special treat.

Chelsea Buns

Preparation time:
20 minutes + 1 hour
20 minutes standing
Total cooking time:
20 minutes
Makes 24

1/4 oz sachet dried yeast
1 teaspoon sugar
1 tablespoon all-purpose flour
1/2 cup milk, warmed
2 1/2 cups all-purpose flour, sifted
4 oz butter, chopped
1 tablespoon sugar
1/2 teaspoon pumpkin pie spice
1 egg, lightly beaten
2 teaspoons grated lemon rind
2 oz butter, extra
1/4 cup light brown sugar
1 cup mixed dried fruit
1/2 teaspoon pumpkin pie spice, extra

Glaze
1 tablespoon milk
2 tablespoons sugar

1. Line 12 x 10 x 3/4 inch shallow jelly roll pan with waxed paper. Combine yeast, sugar and flour in a mixing bowl. Gradually add milk; blend until smooth. Stand bowl, covered with plastic wrap, in warm place 10 minutes or until foamy.
2. Place flour, butter, sugar and spice in food processor bowl. Using the pulse action, press button for 30 seconds. Add egg, rind and yeast mixture and process for 15 seconds or until it almost forms a dough.
3. Turn onto lightly floured surface, knead for 2 minutes or until dough is smooth; shape into a ball. Place in a lightly oiled mixing bowl. Leave, covered

Chelsea Buns (left) and Chocolate Gateau (page 4).

with plastic wrap, in warm place for 1 hour or until well risen. Knead dough again 2 minutes or until smooth.
4. Preheat oven to moderately hot 415°F. Using electric beaters, beat extra butter and the sugar in small mixing bowl until light and creamy. Roll dough out to 16 x 14 inch rectangle. Spread butter and sugar mixture all over the dough to within 3/4 inch of edge of one of the longer sides. Sprinkle with combined fruit and extra spice.
5. Roll dough lengthways, firmly and evenly, into a log, jelly roll style, to enclose fruit and butter mixture. Using a sharp knife, cut roll into 24 slices. Arrange slices evenly apart on prepared pan. Leave, covered with plastic wrap, in warm place for 10 minutes or until well risen.
6. Bake buns for 20 minutes or until well browned and cooked through. Remove from oven; brush liberally with glaze. Transfer to wire rack to cool.
7. *To make Glaze:* Combine milk and sugar in pan. Stir over low heat until sugar dissolves and mixture is almost boiling. Remove from heat.

Chocolate Gateau

Preparation time:
  40 minutes
Total cooking time:
  30 minutes
Makes 9 inch cake

2 cups sugar
2 cups water
8 oz unsalted butter
1/2 cup cocoa powder
1 teaspoon baking soda
3 cups self-rising flour
4 eggs, lightly beaten

Mock Cream
1/2 cup sugar
1/2 cup water
8 oz unsalted butter, softened

Chocolate Icing
3 oz dark chocolate, chopped
1/2 oz butter
2 oz white chocolate, chopped

1. Preheat oven to a moderate 350°F. Brush two 9 inch shallow round cake pans with melted butter or oil. Line base and sides with waxed paper; grease paper.
2. Combine sugar, water, butter, cocoa and soda in large pan. Stir over low heat until mixture comes to the boil, reduce heat and simmer for 3 minutes.

Transfer mixture to large mixing bowl, cool to lukewarm.
3. Stir in sifted flour and eggs. Beat with wooden spoon until just combined; do not overbeat. Pour mixture into prepared pans; smooth surface. Bake 30 minutes or until skewer comes out clean when inserted into center of cake. Stand cake in pan 3 minutes before turning onto wire rack to cool.
4. *To make Mock Cream:* Combine sugar and water in small pan. Stir constantly over low heat until sugar has dissolved and mixture boils. Remove from heat; cool. Beat butter in small mixing bowl until light and creamy. Pour cooled syrup in a thin stream over creamed butter, beating constantly for 3–4 minutes or until glossy and smooth.
5. *To make Chocolate Icing:* Combine dark chocolate and butter in a pan. Stir constantly over low heat until chocolate melts; remove from heat. Spread chocolate evenly over top layer of cake. Melt white chocolate in same way as dark chocolate. Place into small paper decorating bag, seal open end. Snip tip off decoratating bag; drizzle chocolate decoratively over cake.

4

Streusel Teacake.

6. To assemble cake:
Place plain cake layer on a serving plate. Spread cake evenly with half of the mock cream. Pipe an edge around rim of cake with remaining mock cream. Place iced layer on top.

Note: Decorated cake can be made day before required. Do not refrigerate. Cover and store in cool place.

Streusel Teacake

Preparation time:
  30 minutes
Total cooking time:
  25 minutes
Makes 7 1/2 inch round cake

1 egg
1/2 cup sugar
1/2 cup milk
1 cup self-rising flour
4 oz unsalted butter,
  melted

Streusel Layer
1/2 cup all-purpose flour
2 oz unsalted butter
1/4 cup light brown sugar

Topping
1 oz unsalted butter,
  melted
1 teaspoon ground
  cinnamon
1 tablespoon sugar

1. Preheat oven to moderate 350°F. Brush a deep round 6 3/4 inch cake pan with melted butter or oil.

5

2. Using electric beaters, beat egg in small mixing bowl for 5 minutes or until thick and pale. Add sugar gradually, beating constantly until dissolved and mixture is pale yellow and glossy.

3. Stir in milk. Using a metal spoon, fold in sifted flour and melted butter quickly and lightly.

4. *To make Streusel Layer:* Sift flour into medium bowl, add chopped butter and sugar. Using fingertips, rub butter into flour for 2 minutes or until the mixture is fine and crumbly.

5. Spread half cake mixture into prepared pan; sprinkle over streusel layer and spread remaining cake mixture over. Bake for 25 minutes or until skewer comes out clean when inserted into center of cake. Stand cake in pan 5 minutes before turning out on wire rack to cool.

For Topping: Brush cake with melted butter and sprinkle with combined cinnamon and sugar.

Cranberry Muffins

Preparation time:
  20 minutes
Total cooking time:
  20 minutes
Makes 12

2 1/2 cups self-rising
  flour
2/3 cup sugar
1/4 cup chopped pecan
  nuts
1 teaspoon finely grated
  lemon rind
1 egg, lightly beaten
1 cup milk
3 oz butter, melted
1/2 cup whole cranberry
  sauce

1. Preheat oven to moderately hot 415°F. Brush melted butter or oil into 12 muffin cups (1/3-cup capacity). Sift flour into a large mixing bowl. Add sugar, pecans and lemon rind, stir until combined. Make a well in the center.

2. Combine egg, milk and butter in a small mixing bowl, add all at once to dry ingredients. Using a wooden spoon, stir until ingredients are just combined; do not overbeat.

3. Spoon half the mixture into prepared muffin cups. Top each muffin with cranberry sauce. Spoon remaining mixture over cranberry sauce.

4. Bake 20 minutes or until puffed and golden brown. Turn onto wire rack to cool.

Caramel Hazelnut Scrolls

Preparation time:
  20 minutes
Total cooking time:
  25 minutes
Makes 16

2 1/2 cups self-rising
  flour
1/2 cup sugar
4 oz butter
1/2 cup milk
1/4 cup sour cream
2 oz butter, extra,
  softened
1/3 cup light brown
  sugar, firmly packed
1/3 cup chopped
  hazelnuts

Caramel Icing
1 1/4 oz butter
1/4 cup light brown
  sugar, firmly packed
1 tablespoon milk
1/2 cup confectioners'
  sugar, sifted

1. Preheat oven to moderately hot 415°F. Brush a shallow 9 inch square cake pan with melted butter. Sift flour into a large mixing bowl; add sugar and butter. Using fingertips, rub butter into flour for 2 minutes or until the mixture is fine and crumbly.

Cranberry Muffins (top) and Caramel Hazelnut Scrolls.

Add combined milk and sour cream to bowl, stir until ingredients are just combined and the mixture almost smooth. **2.** Turn dough onto lightly floured surface. Knead for 1 minute or until smooth. Roll out dough on lightly floured surface to a 16 x 12 inch rectangle. Combine extra butter, brown sugar and hazelnuts in mixing bowl. Crumble mixture evenly over dough. **3.** Roll dough from the long side into a log, jelly roll style. Using a sharp knife, cut into 16 even slices. Place slices in prepared pan. Bake for 25 minutes or until cakes sound hollow when tapped. Turn onto a wire rack, turn right side up. **4. *To make Caramel Icing:*** Melt butter in a small saucepan, add brown sugar and milk. Stir over low heat for 1 minute or until bubbly. Add sifted confectioners' sugar, stir over low heat for 1 minute or until mixture is smooth. Spread cake with caramel icing while icing and cake are still hot, allow to cool. Sprinkle with extra chopped hazelnuts, if you like.

7

Stand yeast mixture in warm place for 10 minutes or until foamy.

Add milk, egg, butter and yeast to flour and mix to dough with a knife.

English Muffins

Preparation time:
  20 minutes + 1 hour
  40 minutes standing
Total cooking time:
  16 minutes
Makes 15

1/4 oz sachet dried yeast
1/2 teaspoon sugar
1 teaspoon all-purpose
  flour
1/4 cup warm water
4 cups all-purpose flour,
  extra
1 teaspoon salt
1 1/3 cups lukewarm milk
1 egg, lightly beaten
1 1/4 oz butter, melted

1. Lightly dust two 13 x 11 inch baking sheets with flour. Combine yeast, sugar, flour and water in bowl; blend until smooth. Leave, covered with plastic wrap, in a warm place 10 minutes or until foamy. Sift extra flour and salt into large bowl. **2.** Make a well in center, add milk, egg, butter and yeast mixture. Using a knife, mix to a soft dough. **3.** Turn dough onto lightly floured surface, knead for 2 minutes or until smooth. Shape dough into ball, place in large, lightly oiled bowl. Leave, covered with plastic wrap, in warm place 1 1/2 hours or until well risen. **4.** Preheat oven to moderately hot 415°F. Knead dough again for 2 minutes or until smooth. Roll dough to 1/2 inch thickness. Cut into rounds with a 3 inch cutter. Place rounds onto prepared baking sheets. Leave, covered with plastic wrap, in warm place 10 minutes. **5.** Bake muffins for 8 minutes, turn over and bake 8 minutes more.

English Muffins.

Knead dough for 2 minutes or until smooth, shape into a ball.

Roll dough to 1/2 inch thickness, cut into circles with a 3 inch cutter.

Sour Cream Pound Cake

Preparation time:
 10 minutes
Total cooking time:
 30 minutes
Makes 8 inch round cake

3 1/2 oz unsalted butter
2/3 cup sugar
2 eggs, lightly beaten
1/2 teaspoon vanilla
 extract
1 1/4 cups self-rising
 flour, sifted
1/2 cup sour cream

1. Preheat oven to moderate 350°F. Brush a deep 8 inch cake pan with oil, line base with waxed paper; grease paper.
2. Using electric beaters, beat butter and sugar in bowl until creamy. Add eggs gradually, beating well after each addition. Add vanilla; beat until combined.
3. Transfer mixture to large mixing bowl. Using a metal spoon, fold in flour and cream. Stir until just combined and mixture is smooth.
4. Spoon mixture into prepared pan; smooth surface. Bake for 30 minutes or until skewer comes out clean when inserted in center of cake. Turn onto wire rack to cool. Dust with confectioners' sugar.

Devonshire Splits (Cream Buns)

Preparation time:
 30 minutes + 1 hour
 15 minutes standing
Total cooking time:
 20 minutes
Makes 12

3 1/2 cups all-purpose
 flour, sifted
2 tablespoons sugar
pinch salt
1 1/3 cups milk, warmed
2 oz butter, melted
1/4 oz sachet dried yeast
1 1/4 cups cream
1 tablespoon
 confectioners' sugar
1/2 cup raspberry jam
2 tablespoons
 confectioners' sugar,
 extra

1. Line base of a 13 x 11 inch baking sheet with waxed paper; grease paper. Dust pan lightly with flour; shake off excess.
2. Place flour, sugar and salt in food processor bowl. Combine milk and butter in a small bowl. Sprinkle yeast into milk mixture, stir to dissolve. Pour yeast mixture onto dry ingredients.
3. Using the pulse action, press button for 30 seconds or until a soft, smooth dough

forms. Transfer dough to a lightly oiled mixing bowl. Leave, covered with plastic wrap, in warm place for 1 hour or until well risen.
4. Turn dough onto lightly floured surface, knead for 2 minutes or until smooth. Divide into 12 pieces. Knead one at a time on lightly floured surface for 30 seconds, shape into a ball. Repeat process with remaining dough.
5. Preheat oven to moderately hot 415°F. Place balls of dough evenly apart on prepared baking sheet. Leave, covered with plastic wrap, in warm place for 15 minutes or until well risen. Bake 20 minutes or until well browned and cooked through. Stand for 5 minutes before transferring to wire rack to cool.
6. Using a serrated knife, split each bun in half, but do not cut all the way through. Using electric beaters, beat cream and sugar in small mixing bowl until firm peaks form. Fill the buns with the whipped cream and jam. Dust with confectioners' sugar before serving.

Note: Best filled close to serving time.

*Devonshire Splits (top) and
Sour Cream Pound Cake.*

Mini Lemon Griddle Cakes

Preparation time:
  10 minutes
Total cooking time:
  4 minutes per batch
Makes about 25

1 cup self-rising flour
$^1/3$ cup sugar
2 teaspoons finely
  grated lemon rind
1 egg, lightly beaten
$^1/2$ cup milk
$^1/3$ cup lemon butter
$^3/4$ cup cream,
  whipped

1. Sift flour into a medium mixing bowl, add sugar and lemon rind, stir until combined; make a well in the center.
2. Combine egg and milk in a small bowl, add to flour mixture all at once. Using a wooden spoon, stir until all the liquid is incorporated and batter is free of lumps.
3. Brush base of a frying pan lightly with melted butter. Drop heaped teaspoonfuls of mixture onto base of pan about 1$^1/4$ inches apart. Cook over medium heat 2 minutes or until underside is golden. Turn cakes over and cook other side.
4. Remove from pan; repeat process with remaining mixture.

Serve topped with lemon butter and whipped cream.

Note: If the pan is too hot or over-greased, surface of griddle cakes will be uneven.

Cherry Ripple Teacake

Preparation time:
  30 minutes
Total cooking time:
  35–40 minutes
Makes 8 inch ring cake

1$^1/2$ lb jar pitted cherries
1 tablespoon
  cornstarch
2 cups self-rising flour
$^3/4$ cup sugar
$^1/3$ cup shredded
  coconut
4 oz butter, chopped
1 egg
$^3/4$ cup milk

1. Preheat oven to moderate 350°F. Brush an 8 inch ring pan with melted butter or oil. Line base and sides with waxed paper; grease paper. Drain the cherries and reserve half a cup of syrup.
2. Place cherries into medium pan, blend cornstarch with reserved syrup, add to cherries. Stir over low heat until mixture boils and thickens. Set aside to cool.
3. Sift flour into large mixing bowl; add sugar, coconut and butter. Using fingertips, rub butter into flour mixture for 2–3 minutes or until mixture is fine and crumbly. Measure out half cup of mixture and reserve for top.
4. Add combined egg and milk to bowl and stir until mixture is almost smooth. Spoon two-thirds of mixture into prepared pan; smooth surface. Carefully spoon on cooled cherry mixture. Spoon remaining mixture in small mounds on top of surface, sprinkle over reserved half cup flour mixture.
5. Bake for 35–40 minutes or until a skewer comes out clean when inserted into center of cake. Stand cake in pan 10 minutes before turning onto wire rack to cool.

Note: Any canned berries can be used.

Cherry Ripple Teacake (top)
and Mini Lemon Griddle Cakes.

Chocolate Raspberry Jelly Roll

Preparation time:
25 minutes
Total cooking time:
12–15 minutes
Makes one jelly roll

1/2 cup self-rising flour
1/4 cup cocoa powder
3 eggs
1/2 cup sugar
1/4 cup grated dark
  chocolate
1 tablespoon hot water
1 tablespoon sugar, extra
1 1/4 cups cream, lightly
  whipped
1 packet frozen
  raspberries

1. Preheat oven to moderate 350°F. Brush a 12 x 10 x 3/4 inch jelly roll pan with oil. Line base and two sides with waxed paper; grease paper. Sift flour and cocoa three times onto waxed paper.

2. Using electric beaters, beat eggs in bowl for 4–5 minutes or until thick and pale. Add sugar gradually, beating constantly until mixture is pale, yellow and glossy. Transfer mixture to large bowl.

3. Using a metal spoon, fold in sifted flour, cocoa, chocolate and water quickly and lightly. Spread mixture evenly into pan; smooth surface. Bake 12–15 minutes, until lightly golden and springy.

4. Place sheet of waxed paper on a dry dish towel. Sprinkle with extra sugar. Turn cake onto paper; stand 2 minutes. Carefully roll cake up with paper; stand 5 minutes. Unroll cake, discard paper. spread with whipped cream and raspberries; reroll. Trim ends of roll.

Chocolate Raspberry Jelly Roll.

Brush jelly roll pan with oil, line base and sides with waxed paper, grease paper.

Using electric beaters, beat eggs, then add sugar gradually.

Fold in sifted flour, cocoa, chocolate and water with a metal spoon.

On dry dish towel, sprinkle paper with sugar and roll up cake.

Orange Fig Cake

Preparation time:
  15 minutes
Total cooking time:
  1 hour 10 minutes
Makes 8 inch round cake

4 oz butter
$^1/_2$ cup light brown sugar
$^1/_2$ cup honey
3 eggs, lightly beaten
$^1/_2$ cup chopped dried
  figs
2 teaspoons finely
  grated orange rind
1 small orange, peeled,
  chopped
$^1/_2$ cup oat bran
1 cup self-rising
  flour
$^1/_4$ cup milk

1. Preheat oven to moderately slow 315°F. Brush a deep, 8 inch round cake pan with melted butter or oil, line base with waxed paper; grease paper. Using electric beaters, beat butter, sugar and honey in a small bowl until light and creamy. Add eggs gradually, beating after each addition.
2. Transfer mixture to large bowl; add figs, orange rind and orange, oat bran, sifted flour and milk. Using a metal spoon, stir until mixture is combined.

3. Pour mixture into prepared pan; smooth surface. Bake for 1 hour 10 minutes or until a skewer comes out clean when inserted in center of cake. Leave cake in pan 5 minutes before turning onto wire rack to cool. Dust with confectioners' sugar.

Hazelnut and Coffee Cream Gateau

Preparation time:
  30 minutes
Total cooking time:
  20 minutes
Makes 8 inch round double layer cake

$^2/_3$ cup self-rising flour
$^1/_3$ cup cornstarch
4 eggs
$^2/_3$ cup sugar
1 tablespoon instant
  coffee powder
1 tablespoon hot water
$^1/_4$ cup ground
  hazelnuts
$^1/_4$ teaspoon ground
  cinnamon, for dusting

Filling
1 cup cream
$^1/_4$ cup confectioners'
  sugar
1 teaspoon instant
  coffee powder, extra
1 teaspoon hot water,
  extra

1. Preheat oven to moderate 350°F. Brush two shallow 8 inch round cake pans with melted butter or oil. Line base with waxed paper; grease paper. Dust pans lightly with flour, shake off excess. Sift flour and cornstarch three times onto waxed paper.
2. Using electric beaters, beat eggs in small mixing bowl for 2 minutes or until thick and pale. Add sugar gradually, beating constantly until dissolved and mixture is pale yellow and glossy. Transfer mixture to large mixing bowl.
3. Using a metal spoon, fold in combined coffee and water, hazelnuts and flours quickly and lightly.
4. Spread mixture evenly in prepared pans. Bake for 20 minutes or until sponges are lightly golden and shrink from side of the pans. Turn onto wire rack to cool.
5. *To make Filling:* Using electric beaters, beat cream, confectioners' sugar and combined extra coffee and water in small mixing bowl until soft peaks form.
6. Place first cake layer on a board. Spread with filling. Place remaining cake on top. Transfer to serving plate. Dust with cinnamon.

Hazelnut and Coffee Cream Gateau (top) and Orange Fig Cake.

Cherry, Date and Walnut Roll

Preparation time:
  15 minutes
Total cooking time:
  50 minutes + 15
  minutes standing
Makes one nut roll

1/2 *cup finely chopped*
  fresh dates
2 *tablespoons currants*
1/3 *cup water*
1/3 *cup light brown sugar*
1 1/4 *oz butter*
1/2 *teaspoon baking soda*
1/2 *cup chopped walnuts*
1/4 *cup chopped glacé*
  cherries
1/2 *teaspoon ground*
  nutmeg
1 *egg, lightly beaten*
3/4 *cup self-rising flour,*
  sifted

1. Preheat oven to
moderate 350°F. Brush
an 8 x 3 inch bread mold
(4-cup capacity) with
melted butter or oil.
2. Place dates, currants,
water, sugar and butter in
small pan. Stir over low
heat 5 minutes or until
butter has melted and
mixture boils. Remove
pan from heat, cool
slightly. Add soda; stir.
3. Place walnuts, cherries,
nutmeg, egg, flour and
date mixture into mixing
bowl. Stir with a wooden
spoon until combined.

4. Spoon mixture into
prepared mold; close
open end of mold with
lid. Lay mold on its side
in oven, bake 45 minutes.
Leave cake in mold
15 minutes before
transferring to wire
rack to cool.

Note: Bread molds are
shaped tin cannisters
with lids on both ends.
They can be found in
specialty kitchen stores.

> HINT
> Serve roll cut into
> slices spread with
> cream cheese or your
> favorite fruit butter.

Lemon and Pecan Syrup Loaf

Preparation time:
  15 minutes
Total cooking time:
  45 minutes
Makes 10 x 6 x
2 1/4 *inch loaf*

1 1/4 *cups self-rising*
  flour
4 *oz unsalted butter,*
  chopped
3/4 *cup sugar*
2 *eggs*
1/3 *cup milk*
1/2 *cup coarsely*
  chopped pecan nuts
1 *tablespoon grated*
  lemon rind

Lemon Syrup
1/4 *cup lemon juice*
2 *tablespoons water*
1/2 *cup sugar*
1 3/4 *oz butter*

1. Preheat oven to
moderate 350°F. Brush
a 10 x 6 x 2 1/4 inch loaf
pan with melted butter
or oil. Cover base and
two sides with waxed

Lemon and Pecan Syrup Loaf (left)
and Cherry, Date and Walnut Roll.

paper; grease paper.

2. Place flour in food processor bowl; add butter and sugar. Using the pulse action, press button for 20 seconds or until mixture is fine and crumbly.

3. Add combined eggs and milk to bowl, process 10 seconds or until just combined. Add nuts and rind, process 5 seconds. Spoon mixture into prepared pan; smooth surface. Bake for 45 minutes or until skewer comes out clean when inserted in center of cake. Leave cake in the pan.

4. *To make Lemon Syrup:* Place juice, water, sugar and butter in a small pan. Stir over medium heat for 2 minutes or until sugar has dissolved and mixture boils. Reduce heat, simmer, uncovered, 3 minutes. Pour cooled lemon syrup over the hot cake or hot syrup over cooled cake in pan.

Buttermilk Scones

Preparation time:
  15 minutes
Total cooking time:
  10–12 minutes
Makes 12

2 cups self-rising flour
1 tablespoon sugar
2 oz butter
³/4 cup buttermilk or
  ¹/2 cup milk and
  ¹/4 cup sour cream
jam and whipped cream
  to serve

1. Preheat oven to moderate 350°F. Dust a 12 x 11 inch baking sheet lightly with flour.
2. Sift flour and sugar into large mixing bowl; add chopped butter.
3. Using fingertips, rub butter into flour for 1 minute or until mixture is fine and crumbly. Add buttermilk, stir until a soft dough is formed.
4. Turn out onto lightly floured surface and knead lightly until dough is no longer sticky. Press dough to ¹/2 inch in thickness. Cut into rounds, with plain or fluted 2 inch cutter.
5. Place rounds just touching on prepared baking sheet. Bake for 10–12 minutes or until golden brown.
6. Serve scones warm with apricot or strawberry jam and lightly whipped cream.

Crumpets

Preparation time:
  25 minutes + 1 hour
  25 minutes
Total cooking time:
  6 minutes
Makes 12–14

¹/4 oz sachet dried yeast
1 teaspoon sugar
1³/4 cups warm water
3 cups all-purpose flour
2 tablespoons
  powdered milk
1 teaspoon baking soda
2 tablespoons warm
  water
1 oz butter, melted

1. Combine yeast, sugar and water in medium mixing bowl. Leave, covered with plastic wrap, in warm place for about 10 minutes or until foamy.
2. Sift flour and powdered milk into large mixing bowl. Make a well in the center, add yeast mixture. Using a wooden spoon, mix to a soft dough. Leave, covered, in a warm place for 1 hour or until well risen and surface is bubbly.
3. Add combined baking soda and warm water, stir well. Stand mixture for 15 minutes.
4. Lightly brush a large frying pan with melted butter. Place greased egg rings in pan. Place

enough mixture in each ring to come to top of ring. Cook over medium heat for 4–5 minutes or until bubbles appear on top.
5. Remove ring, turn crumpet over, cook 30 seconds. Remove from pan. Toast crumpets, serve.

Easy Sponge with Jam and Cream

Preparation time:
  15 minutes
Total cooking time:
  20 minutes + 5
  minutes standing
*Makes 8 inch round
double layer cake*

¹/2 cup all-purpose flour
¹/4 cup cornstarch
3 eggs
¹/3 cup sugar
1 oz butter, melted
¹/2 teaspoon vanilla
  extract
2 tablespoons raspberry
  jam
²/3 cup cream
1 tablespoon
  confectioners' sugar
2 tablespoons
  confectioners' sugar,
  extra

1. Preheat oven to moderate 350°F. Brush two shallow 8 inch round cake pans with oil. Line base with waxed paper; grease paper. Dust pans lightly with flour; shake off excess.

Clockwise from left: Buttermilk Scones, Easy Sponge with Jam and Cream, Crumpets.

2. Sift flour and cornstarch three times onto waxed paper. Place eggs in a small mixing bowl. Using electric beaters, beat eggs on high speed for 2 minutes. Add sugar gradually, beating constantly 8 minutes or until dissolved and the mixture is pale yellow and glossy.

3. Transfer mixture to large mixing bowl. Using a metal spoon, fold in butter, vanilla and flours quickly and lightly. Spread mixture evenly into prepared pans. Bake 20 minutes or until sponges are lightly golden and shrink from side of pan. Remove from oven. Leave in pans for 5 minutes before turning onto wire rack.

4. Spread jam over one sponge layer. Beat cream and confectioners' sugar with electric beaters until firm peaks form. Spread cream over jam. Top with remaining sponge layer. Dust sponge with extra confectioners' sugar.

21

Orange Bun

Preparation time:
45 minutes + 1 hour
5 minutes standing
Total cooking time:
20 minutes
*Makes 9 inch round
with eight wedges*

2 cups all-purpose flour
1/4 oz sachet dried yeast
1/3 cup chopped mixed
   candied citrus peel
2 tablespoons sugar
2 teaspoons grated
   orange rind
1/3 cup warm milk
1/3 cup orange juice
1 egg, lightly beaten
1 oz butter, melted

Glaze
1 tablespoon water
1 teaspoon sugar
1 teaspoon gelatin

1. Brush a deep 9 inch
round cake pan with
melted butter or oil. Sift
flour into a large mixing
bowl. Add yeast, mixed
peel, sugar and orange
rind, stir until combined.
Make a well in the center.
2. Combine milk, orange
juice, egg and butter in a
small mixing bowl, add
to flour mixture. Using
a knife, mix to a soft
dough. Turn onto lightly
floured surface, knead
for 10 minutes or until
dough is smooth and
elastic. To test, press a

finger into the dough.
When ready, the
dough will spring back
immediately and not
leave an indent.
3. Place dough into
a large, lightly oiled
mixing bowl. Leave,
covered with plastic
wrap, in warm place
for 45 minutes or
until well risen.
4. Knead dough again
for 1 minute or until
smooth. Press dough
into prepared cake pan.
Leave, covered with
plastic wrap, in warm
place for 20 minutes or
until well risen.
5. Preheat oven to
moderate 350°F. Cut
dough into eight
wedges by carefully
making deep cuts with
a sharp pointed, oiled
knife. Be careful not to
push out all the air. If
the dough deflates,
simply leave for another
5 minutes or until risen.
6. Bake for 20 minutes
or until golden brown
and cooked through.
Dough should sound
hollow when tapped.
Turn onto wire rack.
7. *To make Glaze:*
Combine water, sugar
and gelatin in a small
mixing bowl. Place
over a pan of
simmering water,
until sugar and
gelatin are dissolved.
Brush over bun while
still hot.

Lemon Banana Cake

Preparation time:
20 minutes
Total cooking time:
45 minutes
*Makes 8 inch ring
cake*

1 1/2 cups self-rising
   flour
3 oz butter, softened
1/2 cup sugar
1/2 cup shredded
   coconut

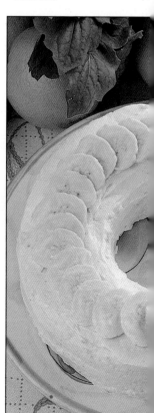

Lemon Banana Cake (left) and Orange Bun.

22

2 teaspoons grated
  lemon rind
1/3 cup lemon juice
2 eggs, lightly beaten
3/4 cup mashed, ripe
  banana

Cream Cheese Icing
3 oz cream cheese
1 1/2 oz butter, softened
1/3 cup confectioners'
  sugar
1 teaspoon grated
  lemon rind

1. Preheat oven to moderate 350°F. Brush an 8 inch ring pan with oil, dust lightly with flour, shake off excess.
2. Sift flour into a large mixing bowl. Add butter, sugar, coconut, lemon rind and juice, eggs and banana.
3. Using electric beaters, beat on low speed for 1 minute or until ingredients are just moistened. Beat on high speed for 2 minutes or until well combined and increased in volume.
4. Pour mixture evenly into prepared pan; smooth surface. Bake for 45 minutes or until lightly golden and a skewer comes out clean when inserted in cake.
5. Leave cake in pan for 3 minutes before turning onto wire rack to cool.
6. *To make Cream Cheese Icing:* Beat cream cheese and butter in small mixing bowl until light and creamy. Add confectioners' sugar and lemon rind, beating for 2 minutes or until the mixture is smooth.
7. Spread icing onto cooled cake.

23

Treacle and Malt Loaf

Preparation time:
  15 minutes + 1 hour
  50 minutes standing
Total cooking time:
  40 minutes
Makes 1 loaf

1 cup lukewarm water
1/4 oz sachet dried yeast
1 teaspoon sugar
2 cups plain whole
  wheat flour
1 cup all-purpose flour
2 teaspoons ground
  cinnamon
1/2 cup raisins
1 oz butter, melted
1 tablespoon treacle
1 tablespoon barley malt
1 tablespoon hot milk
1/2 teaspoon malt, extra

1. Brush 8 1/2 x
5 1/2 x 2 3/4 inch loaf
pan with oil.
2. Combine water,
yeast and sugar in small
bowl. Leave in warm
position for 10 minutes
or until foamy.
3. Sift flours and
cinnamon into large
mixing bowl, add
raisins, stir to combine.
Make a well in center.
Add melted butter,
treacle, malt and yeast
mixture. Using a knife,
mix to a soft dough.
4. Turn dough onto
lightly floured surface.
Knead for 4 minutes or
until smooth. Shape
dough into ball, place

into lightly oiled mixing
bowl. Leave, covered
with plastic wrap, in
warm place for 1 hour
or until well risen.
5. Punch dough with
fist. Knead for 3 minutes
or until smooth.
6. Arrange dough into
pan. Leave, covered
with plastic, in warm
place 40 minutes or
until well risen. Brush
with combined milk
and malt. Heat oven to
moderate 350°F. Bake
40 minutes or until well
browned and cooked
through. Leave in pan
for 3 minutes before
transferring to wire
rack to cool.

Note: This loaf is best
eaten on day of baking.
However, it can be
frozen for a month.

Sacher Slice

Preparation time:
  15 minutes
Total cooking time:
  40 minutes + 30
  minutes refrigeration
Makes 12 x 8 inch slice

5 oz dark chocolate,
  finely chopped
2 tablespoons
  chocolate-flavored
  liqueur
4 oz butter
1/2 cup sugar
4 eggs, separated
1/2 cup self-rising flour
1/2 cup all-purpose flour

Icing
6 oz dark chocolate,
  finely chopped
4 oz butter
1 teaspoon chocolate-
  flavored liqueur, extra

1. Preheat oven to
moderate 350°F. Brush
a shallow rectangular
12 x 8 inch cake pan
with melted butter or
oil. Line base and two
sides with waxed paper;
grease paper.
2. Place chocolate
in small bowl. Stand
bowl over simmering
water and stir until
chocolate is melted and
smooth. Cool slightly,
stir in liqueur.
3. Using electric
beaters, beat butter and
sugar in small mixing
bowl until light and
creamy. Add egg yolks
gradually, beating
thoroughly after each
addition. Transfer
mixture to large mixing
bowl, stir in chocolate.
Using metal spoon,
fold in sifted flours.
4. Place egg whites
in small, clean, dry
mixing bowl. Using
electric beaters, beat
until soft peaks form.
Using large metal
spoon, fold egg whites
into cake mixture.
5. Spoon mixture into
prepared pan. Bake for
35 minutes or until a
skewer comes out clean
when inserted into the
center of slice. Leave
in pan for 5 minutes

Treacle and Malt Loaf (left) and Sacher Slice.

before turning onto wire rack to cool.
6. *To make Icing:* Place chocolate, butter and liqueur in medium heatproof bowl. Stand bowl over pan of simmering water, stir until chocolate has melted and mixture is smooth. Cool for 10–15 minutes or until icing is thick enough to spread evenly over cake, using a flat-bladed knife. Refrigerate for 30 minutes before transferring to plate for serving.

Note: Sacher Slice can be split in the middle and spread with apricot or plum jam. It is also good as a dessert, with cream or ice-cream. It can be stored, in an airtight container, for two to three days in a cool, dry place.

Morsels

For morning coffee, a church supper or more casual get-together, you'll find these easy-to-handle sweet tastes just the thing. They're ideal for bake sales and cake stalls, too, and if there should be any leftovers, they will prove a popular addition to lunchboxes.

Pithiviers

Preparation time:
  20 minutes
Total cooking time:
  20 minutes
Makes one 9 inch round

2 sheets ready-made
  puff pastry
1 egg, lightly beaten
1 tablespoon
  confectioners' sugar

Filling
3 oz butter, softened
$2/3$ cup confectioners'
  sugar, extra
2 egg yolks
$1^1/4$ cups ground
  almonds
2 teaspoons almond
  extract

1. Preheat oven to moderately hot 415°F. Brush a 13 x 11 inch baking sheet with melted butter or oil. Cut a 9 inch round from one sheet of pastry and a 10 inch round from the other. Place the 9 inch round onto baking sheet.
2. *To make Filling:* Using electric beaters, beat butter and extra confectioners' sugar in medium mixing bowl until light and creamy. Add egg yolks, beat until combined. Add almonds and extract, stir until combined.
3. Spread filling over pastry base, leaving a 1 inch border. Place remaining pastry round over top; press slightly on border to seal.
4. Mark into eight curved wedges without cutting all the way through. Make deep cuts around the border at $3/4$ inch intervals.
5. Brush pastry with combined beaten egg and confectioners' sugar. Bake for 20 minutes or until puffed and golden.

From top: Lamingtons and Fruit Tartlets (page 28) and Pithiviers.

Fruit Tartlets

Preparation time:
   20 minutes
Total cooking time:
   40 minutes
Makes 12

12 frozen (unbaked)
   mini tart cases
2 tablespoons custard
   powder
$1/3$ cup cornstarch
$1/3$ cup sugar
1 teaspoon vanilla
   extract
2 egg yolks
$1^1/4$ cups cream
$2/3$ cup milk
12 strawberries
$6^1/2$ oz blueberries

Glaze
1 tablespoon apricot jam
2 tablespoons orange
   juice
2 teaspoons gelatin

1. Preheat oven to
moderate 350°F. Place
frozen tartlets in foil
cases on baking sheet.
Bake 25 minutes or
until golden and
cooked through. Cool.
2. Place custard
powder, cornstarch,
sugar, vanilla and yolks
into medium mixing
bowl. Whisk together
until mixture is smooth
and pale. Heat cream
and milk in pan until
almost boiling; remove
from heat.
3. Add milk gradually
to custard mixture,
whisking constantly.
Strain mixture into pan.
Stir constantly with a
wooden spoon over
medium heat 8 minutes
or until custard boils
and thickens. Remove
from heat. Place plastic
wrap over custard
surface; cool.
4. Divide custard mixture
evenly between the tart
cases. Using a flat-bladed
knife, shape mixture into
a mound; smooth
surface. Decorate with
fruit. Brush with glaze.
5. ***To make Glaze:***
Combine jam, juice and
gelatin in small pan. Stir
over low heat 2 minutes
or until gelatin dissolves
and mixture boils.
Remove from heat;
strain, cool slightly.

Lamingtons

Preparation time:
   1 hour
Total cooking time:
   30 minutes
Makes 16 lamingtons

1 cup self-rising flour
4 eggs
$3/4$ cup sugar
$1/3$ cup milk
1 oz butter

Icing
4 cups confectioners'
   sugar, sifted
$1/2$ cup cocoa powder
$1/2$ cup water
4 cups shredded
   coconut

1. Preheat oven to
moderate 350°F. Brush
a 12 x 8 inch shallow
rectangular cake pan
with melted butter or
oil. Line base and two
sides with waxed
paper; grease paper.
Sift flour three times
onto waxed paper.
2. Using electric beaters,
beat eggs in small mixing
bowl for 10 minutes
or until thick and pale.
Add sugar gradually,
beating constantly until
sugar is dissolved and
mixture is pale yellow
and glossy. Transfer
mixture to large bowl.
3. Place milk and butter
in small pan. Heat over
low heat until butter
is melted.
4. Using large metal
spoon, fold flour into
egg mixture quickly and
lightly. Fold in hot milk
and butter.
5. Spread mixture
evenly into prepared
pan. Bake for 30 minutes
or until cake is lightly
golden and shrinks away
from side of pan. Stand
cake in pan for 5 minutes
before turning out on
wire rack to cool.
6. Carefully trim outer
edges of cake and cut
into 16 even pieces.
7. ***To make Icing:***
Combine sifted
confectioners' sugar
and cocoa and
sufficient liquid in a
medium bowl to form
a firm paste. Stand
bowl over pan of

Banana and Raisin Muffins.

simmering water, stirring until icing is smooth and glossy; remove from heat.
8. Dip each piece of cake into icing and hold over bowl to allow excess icing to drain back into bowl. Place immediately into bowl of coconut and toss gently to ensure cake is completely covered. Stand cakes on wire rack for 20 minutes or until icing is dry.

Note: It is best to make the lamington cake the day before cutting and icing it.

Banana and Raisin Muffins

Preparation time:
  15 minutes
Total cooking time:
  15 minutes
Makes 18

2 cups self-rising
  flour
1 cup oat bran
3/4 cup sugar
4 oz butter, melted
1 cup milk
2 eggs, lightly beaten
1 cup (2 medium)
  mashed, ripe banana
1/3 cup chopped
  raisins

1. Preheat oven to moderately hot 415°F. Brush oil into 18 muffin cups (1/3 cup capacity). Sift flour into mixing bowl. Add oat bran and sugar. Make well in center.
2. Combine butter, milk, eggs, banana and raisins in a small bowl. Add to dry ingredients all at once. Using a wooden spoon, stir until just mixed; do not overbeat.
3. Spoon mixture into prepared muffin pan, filling two-thirds full. Bake for 15 minutes or until puffed and golden brown. Turn onto wire rack to cool.

Cream Horns

Preparation time:
  20 minutes
Total cooking time:
  30 minutes
Makes 8

12 oz ready-made puff
  pastry
1 egg white, lightly
  beaten
1 tablespoon sugar
1/4 cup strawberry
  jam

Custard Cream
1/2 cup milk powder
1/4 cup sugar
1/4 cup custard powder
11/4 cups water
1/3 cup cream

1. Preheat oven to
hot 475°F. Line two
13 x 11 inch cookie
sheets with waxed paper.
Brush eight cream horn
molds with melted
butter or oil.
2. Roll pastry on
lightly floured surface
to 20 x 8 inches
rectangle. Using a
sharp knife, cut pastry
lengthways into eight
1 inch-wide strips.
3. Beginning at the
narrow end of mold,
wrap a strip of pastry
over the mold,
overlapping slightly
each time until you
reach the end. Brush
the pastry lightly with
the egg white; sprinkle
with sugar. Place onto a

prepared cookie sheet.
Repeat process with
remaining pastry.
4. Bake 20 minutes.
Reduce heat to 415°F,
bake further 10 minutes
or until well browned
and puffed. Leave horns
on cookie sheets for
5 minutes. Carefully
twist to remove molds
from horns. Transfer
horns to wire rack
to cool.
5. *To make Custard
Cream:* Place milk
powder, sugar and
custard powder into
small pan. Gradually
add water, blend with
a whisk until smooth.
Whisk over low heat
10 minutes or until
mixture boils and
thickens; remove from
heat. Cover with plastic
wrap; cool. Transfer
mixture to small mixing
bowl. Using electric
beaters, beat custard
and cream on medium
speed 1 minute or until
mixture is thick and
creamy. Custard cream
can be made one day
ahead. Store, covered
with plastic wrap, in
refrigerator. To
assemble, place one
teaspoon jam into base
of each horn. Fill horns
with custard cream.

Vienna Swirls

Preparation time:
  20 minutes
Total cooking time:
  15 minutes
Makes about 20

4 oz butter, softened
1/4 cup sour cream
1/2 cup confectioners'
  sugar
1/2 teaspoon vanilla
  extract
1 cup all-purpose flour
1/4 cup rice flour

1. Preheat oven to
moderate 350°F. Place
paper liners in cups of
two muffin pans. Using
electric beaters, beat
the butter, sour cream,
sifted confectioners'
sugar and vanilla in
a small mixing bowl
until mixture is light
and creamy.
2. Add sifted flour
and rice flour, stir
until combined.
3. Spoon mixture into
a decorating bag fitted
with a star tip; pipe
mixture into prepared
paper liners to one-
third full. Bake for
15 minutes or until
swirls are lightly golden.

Note: A small piece
of glacé cherry can
be placed on the top
of each swirl before
baking, if you like.

Vienna Swirls (top) and Cream Horns.

Add water to flour and butter mixture, stir with knife until just combined.

Roll dough into a rectangle, fold one end over the other; repeat five times.

Passion Fruit Palmiers

Preparation time:
  30 minutes
Total cooking time:
  15 minutes
Makes about 25

2 cups all-purpose flour
1 teaspoon baking
  powder
6 oz cold butter,
  chopped
1/2 cup water
1 tablespoon sugar

Passion Fruit Icing
1 1/2 cups confectioners'
  sugar
1 oz butter, melted
2 passion fruit

1. Preheat oven to moderately hot 415°F. Line two 13 x 11 inch cookie sheets with waxed paper. Sift flour and baking powder into a large mixing bowl.

Add butter, stir until combined. Add water, stir with a knife until just combined. Turn onto lightly floured surface, knead for 1 minute or until smooth.
2. Roll dough to a rectangle approximately 16 x 8 inches. With the short end towards you, fold the end over to two-thirds of the way along the rectangle. Fold the other end back over the top. Turn dough clockwise so the open end is towards you.
3. Roll dough to a rectangle, fold and turn dough as above, five more times. If butter becomes soft, refrigerate dough for 30 minutes, being sure to continue rolling and folding in the same direction.

4. Roll dough on lightly floured surface to a 13 x 12 inch rectangle; trim. Sprinkle with sugar. Fold the long sides to meet in the center. Fold in half lengthways.
5. Using a sharp knife, cut into 1/2 inch slices. Lay slices cut side up on prepared cookie sheets; open slices slightly, brush lightly with water. Bake for 15 minutes or until lightly golden. Transfer to wire rack to cool.
6. *To make Passion Fruit Icing:* Sift confectioners' sugar into a medium mixing bowl, add butter and passion fruit pulp, stir until combined. Spread icing over palmiers.

Note: Be sure to roll, fold and turn the pastry the same way each time so that the layers will all run in the same direction and therefore give a light and crisp result. Store for two days in an airtight container.

Passion Fruit Palmiers.

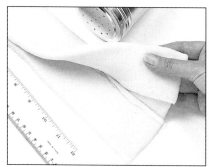

Fold the long sides of dough to meet center. Fold in half lengthways.

To make icing, combine confectioners' sugar, butter and passion fruit pulp.

Mini Fruit Danish

Preparation time:
  40 minutes
Total cooking time:
  15 minutes
Makes 18

2 sheets puff pastry
1/2 cup apricot jam,
  strained
1 tablespoon water

Apricot Filling
1 oz butter, softened
1/4 cup confectioners'
  sugar
1 egg yolk
1/4 cup ground almonds
14 oz can apricot
  halves, drained

1. Preheat oven to
moderately hot 415°F.
Brush two 13 x 11 inch
cookie sheets with
melted butter or oil.

Cut each pastry sheet
into three strips. Cut
each of the strips into
three, to give 18 squares.
**2. *To make Apricot
Filling:*** Using a wooden
spoon, beat butter and
confectioners' sugar in
small bowl until smooth.
Beat egg yolk and
almonds until combined.
3. Divide filling between
the pastry squares,
spread slightly. Place

two apricot halves diagonally onto each square. Bring the remaining two corners of each square over the apricots, press the corners together.

4. Place onto cookie sheets. Bake 15 minutes or until golden brown; remove from oven.

5. Brush with combined jam and water, allow to cool before serving.

Custard Tarts

Preparation time:
  30 minutes + 20
  minutes refrigeration
Total cooking time:
  45 minutes
*Makes twelve 4 inch
tarts*

2 cups all-purpose flour
$^1/_3$ cup rice flour
$^1/_4$ cup confectioners'
  sugar
4 oz butter
1 egg yolk
$^1/_4$ cup iced water
1 egg white, lightly
  beaten

Filling
3 eggs
$1^1/_2$ cups milk
$^1/_4$ cup sugar
1 teaspoon vanilla
  extract
$^1/_2$ teaspoon nutmeg

1. Place flours, confectioners' sugar and butter in food processor bowl. Using the pulse action, press the button for 20 seconds or until the mixture is fine and crumbly. Add egg yolk and almost all water, process 30 seconds or until mixture comes together, adding more water if necessary. Turn onto a lightly floured surface, press together until smooth. Divide

dough into 12 equal portions, roll out and line twelve 4 inch fluted tart pans. Refrigerate 20 minutes.

2. Preheat oven to moderate 350°F. Cut sheets of waxed paper to cover each pastry-lined pan. Spread a layer of dried beans or rice evenly over paper. Place tart pans on a large flat baking sheet and bake 10 minutes. Remove from oven; discard waxed paper and beans/rice. Return to oven and bake a further 10 minutes or until lightly golden. Cool. Brush base and sides of each pastry case with beaten egg white.

3. *To make Filling:* Reduce oven to low 300°F. Combine eggs and milk in a medium mixing bowl, whisk to combine. Add sugar gradually, whisking to dissolve completely. Stir in vanilla. Strain mixture into a jug, then pour into paper liners. Sprinkle with nutmeg and bake for 25 minutes or until filling is just set. Serve tarts at room temperature.

Notes: Be careful not to overcook the tarts as the eggs in the filling will curdle. Ground cinnamon can be used instead of nutmeg.

Custard Tarts (left) and Mini Fruit Danish.

Shortbread

Preparation time:
  20 minutes
Total cooking time:
  35–40 minutes
Makes 24 pieces

8 oz butter
3/4 cup sugar
2 cups all-purpose flour
1/2 cup cornstarch

1. Preheat oven to moderately slow 315°F. Brush an 11 x 7 inch shallow rectangular cake pan with melted butter or oil. Cover base with waxed paper extending over sides; grease paper.
2. Beat butter and sugar in small mixing bowl with electric beaters until light and creamy.
3. Add sifted flours, press together to form a soft dough. Turn onto a lightly floured surface; knead lightly until smooth. Press dough into prepared pan.
4. Score with fingers. Pierce with fork. Bake for 35–40 minutes or until set and browned. When almost cool cut through lines into pieces.

Note: Dough can be rolled out and cut into small rounds or bars. Adjust cooking to suit.

Neenish Tarts

Preparation time:
  25 minutes
Total cooking time:
  Nil
Makes 12

Buttercream
2 oz unsalted butter
1/2 cup confectioners'
  sugar, sifted
1 tablespoon milk
few drops imitation
  rum extract

12 baked mini tart cases
2 tablespoons raspberry
  jam
1 cup confectioners'
  sugar, extra
1 teaspoon vanilla
  extract
3 teaspoons hot water
few drops pink food
  coloring

1. Place butter into small mixing bowl. Using electric beaters, beat on high speed for 1 minute. Add sugar, milk and vanilla, beat until light and creamy.
2. Place 1/2 teaspoon jam into each tartlet; spread over base. Top jam with 2 teaspoons buttercream mixture;

smooth surface with back of a teaspoon.
3. Sift confectioners' sugar into small mixing bowl; make a well in center. Add vanilla and water. Stir until smooth. Divide mixture into two portions. Leave one portion plain and tint the remaining portion pink.
4. Spread 1 teaspoon plain icing over half of each tartlet; allow to set. Spread 1 teaspoon pink icing over remaining half of each tartlet; allow to set.

Coffee Meringue Kisses

Preparation time:
  20 minutes
Total cooking time:
  30 minutes
Makes about 24

3 egg whites
3/4 cup sugar

Filling
4 oz cream cheese
1/2 cup confectioners'
  sugar
2 teaspoons instant
  coffee powder
2 teaspoons hot
  water

1. Preheat oven to slow 300°F. Line two 13 x 11 inch baking sheets with waxed paper.
2. Place egg whites in a small, dry mixing bowl.

From top: Shortbread, Coffee Meringue Kisses and Neenish Tarts.

Using electric beaters, beat egg whites until firm peaks form. Add sugar gradually, beating constantly until mixture is thick and glossy and all sugar is dissolved.
3. Spoon mixture into a decorating bag fitted with a star tip. Pipe meringue onto baking sheets, in mounds about 3/4 inch in diameter.
4. Bake for 30 minutes or until meringues are pale and crisp. Cool completely in the oven, with door slightly ajar.
5. *To make Filling:* Beat cream cheese and confectioners' sugar until light and creamy. Combine coffee and water, stir until dissolved; add to mixture, beat until combined.
6. Spread the base of a meringue with a little filling; join together with another meringue. Repeat with remaining meringues and filling.

HINT
Store meringues in a cool, dark place in an airtight container for up to three days. Fill just before serving. Test that the meringues are dry inside before turning off the oven. If not dry, they will become soft on standing. Soft meringues can be re-crisped in a cool oven.

Bakewell Slice

Preparation time:
  30 minutes
Total cooking time:
  25 minutes
Makes 18

1 cup all-purpose flour
3 oz butter
1 tablespoon sugar
1 tablespoon water
1/2 cup raspberry jam
1/4 cup sliced almonds

Topping
6 oz butter, extra
3/4 cup sugar, extra
3 eggs, lightly beaten
1 cup ground almonds
3/4 cup all-purpose
  flour, extra

1. Preheat oven to moderately hot 415°F. Brush a shallow 11 x 7 x 1 1/4 inch cake pan with melted butter or oil. Cover base and two sides with waxed paper; grease paper.
2. Place sifted flour, butter and sugar into a food processor bowl. Using pulse action, press button for 10 seconds or until mixture is fine and crumbly. Add water, process 5 seconds until mixture is smooth.
3. Turn mixture into prepared pan, press evenly over base using lightly floured hands. Bake for 5 minutes, remove from oven,

allow to cool.
4. *To make Topping:* Using electric beaters, beat extra butter and sugar in small mixing bowl until light and creamy. Add eggs gradually, beating thoroughly after each addition. Transfer mixture to large mixing bowl; add almonds and extra flour. Using a wooden spoon, stir until just combined.
5. Spread pastry base evenly with jam. Spread evenly with topping, sprinkle with almonds. Bake for 20 minutes or until lightly golden, cool in pan. Cut into fingers when cold.

Chocolate Eclairs

Preparation time:
  40 minutes
Total cooking time:
  27 minutes
Makes 10–12 éclairs

1 1/4 oz butter
1/2 cup water
1/2 cup all-purpose
  flour
2 eggs
1 1/4 cups cream,
  whipped
4 oz dark chocolate,
  chopped
3/4 oz butter

1. Preheat oven to moderately hot 415°F. Brush a 13 x 11 inch baking sheet with

Chocolate Eclairs (top) and Bakewell Slice.

melted butter or oil. Combine butter and water in medium pan. Stir over low heat until butter has melted; do not boil. Remove from heat, add flour all at once. Beat until smooth using a wooden spoon. Return to stove, heat until mixture thickens and comes away from side and base of pan. Remove from heat; cool slightly.
2. Transfer mixture to large mixing bowl. Add beaten eggs gradually, beating until mixture is glossy.
3. Spoon mixture into decorating bag fitted with small plain tip. Pipe mixture in 3 inch lengths, 2 inches apart on prepared baking sheet. Bake for 12 minutes. Reduce heat to moderate 350°F. Bake a further 15 minutes or until crisp and brown.
4. Cut éclairs in half lengthways, remove any uncooked mixture.

Return puffs to oven for 4 minutes or until dry. Cool on wire rack.
5. Fill each éclair base with whipped cream, replace tops. Spread each éclair with melted chocolate.
6. *To melt chocolate:* Place chocolate and butter in small heatproof bowl. Stand bowl over pan of simmering water, stir until chocolate has melted and mixture is smooth. Cool slightly.

Stir butter, syrup and sugar over low heat until butter has melted.

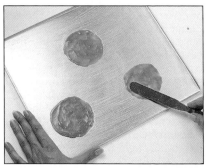

Place teaspoons of mixture on baking sheet, smooth to 3 inch rounds.

Brandy Snap Fans

Preparation time:
 45 minutes
Total cooking time:
 4 minutes each batch
Makes 20

1 oz unsalted butter
2 tablespoons golden
 syrup or dark corn
 syrup
1 tablespoon light
 brown sugar
2 tablespoons all-
 purpose flour, sifted
1 teaspoon ground
 ginger
2 oz dark chocolate,
 melted

1. Preheat oven to moderate 350°F. Brush a 13 x 11 inch baking sheet with melted butter or oil.
2. Combine butter, syrup and sugar in small pan. Stir over low heat until butter has just melted and mixture is smooth; do not boil.
3. Remove pan from heat. Transfer mixture to small bowl. Add flour and ginger. Stir with a wooden spoon until just combined; do not overbeat.
4. Place a level teaspoon of mixture at a time onto prepared baking sheet. Using a flat-bladed knife, spread mixture to make a 3 inch round. (Do not cook more than three at a time.) Bake 4 minutes or until bubbling and lightly browned. Remove baking sheet from oven. Leave rounds on baking sheet for 20 seconds. Carefully loosen edges.
5. Lift round from baking sheet. Beginning from one side of round, quickly pleat or fold towards opposite side in palm of your hand. Pinch folds together at one end to resemble a fan. Repeat process quickly with remaining rounds. Allow to set. Repeat baking and fanning process with remaining mixture.
6. Place melted chocolate into a small bowl. Dip ends of fans into chocolate. Allow to set on wire rack.

HINT
Do not cook more than three rounds at a time; shaping can become difficult as they begin to cool. Instead of making fans, the cooked rounds can be pinched or gathered across the center to resemble a bow, if you prefer.

Brandy Snap Fans.

Pinch folds of cooked round together at one end to make a fan.

Dip open ends of cooled fans into melted chocolate. Allow to set.

Madeleines

Preparation time:
  20 minutes
Total cooking time:
  10–15 minutes
Makes 12

1 cup all-purpose flour
2 eggs
3/4 cup sugar
6 oz unsalted butter,
  melted and cooled
1 teaspoon finely
  grated lemon rind
1/3 cup confectioners'
  sugar

1. Preheat oven to moderate 350°F. Brush madeleine pan cups with melted butter or oil. Dust pans with flour; shake off excess. Sift flour three times onto waxed paper.
2. Combine eggs and sugar in heatproof bowl. Place bowl over pan of simmering water. Beat until mixture is thick and pale yellow. Remove from heat, continue to beat until cooled slightly and increased in volume.
3. Add flour, butter and rind. Using a metal spoon, fold quickly and lightly until ingredients are just combined.
4. Spoon mixture into prepared molds. Bake for 10–12 minutes. Remove; place on wire rack until cold. Dust with confectioners' sugar.

HINT
Madeleine pans are available from specialty kitchenware stores. Muffin top pans may be used instead.

Appel Kuchen Slice

Preparation time:
  20 minutes + 20
  minutes refrigeration
Total cooking time:
  50 minutes
Makes 12 pieces

1 1/3 cups all-purpose
  flour
4 oz butter, chopped
1 tablespoon sugar
1 egg yolk
3 medium green apples,
  peeled and thinly sliced
2 tablespoons sugar
3 teaspoons lemon
  juice
1/2 teaspoon ground
  cinnamon

Topping
1 1/4 cups sour cream
2 tablespoons sugar
1 teaspoon vanilla
  extract
2 eggs, lightly beaten
cinnamon sugar

1. Preheat oven to moderate 350°F. Brush a 12 x 8 inch shallow rectangular cake pan with melted butter or oil. Cover base with waxed paper, extending over two sides; grease paper. Place flour in food processor bowl; add butter and sugar.
2. Using the pulse action, press button for 30 seconds or until mixture is fine and crumbly. Add egg yolk to bowl. Process 10 seconds or until mixture comes together.
3. Press mixture into prepared pan with the back of a spoon; smooth surface. Cover with plastic wrap, refrigerate 20 minutes. Bake pastry 15 minutes. Remove from oven; cool.
4. Place apples, sugar, juice and cinnamon in large bowl; mix well. Arrange apples in overlapping rows over pastry base. Bake 15 minutes. Remove from oven.
To make Topping:
Place sour cream in medium mixing bowl. Beat with a wire whisk until smooth. Add sugar, vanilla and eggs, whisk until well combined. Pour topping over apples; return to oven. Bake further 20 minutes or until topping is set. Cool in pan. Sprinkle with cinnamon sugar before serving. Cut into 12 fingers/bars or diamonds.

Apple Kuchen Slice (top) and Madeleines.

Coconut Almond Macaroons

Preparation time:
  20 minutes
Total cooking time:
  30 minutes
Makes 30

2 eggs, separated
2/3 cup sugar
1/2 teaspoon cream
  of tartar
1 teaspoon vanilla
  extract
1 1/2 cups shredded
  coconut
1 cup sliced almonds

1. Preheat oven to
moderately slow 315°F.
Line a 13 x 7 inch
cookie sheet with
waxed paper. Place egg
whites in a small dry
mixing bowl. Using
electric beaters, beat
the egg whites until
firm peaks form.
2. Add sugar gradually,
beating constantly until
mixture is thick and
glossy and all the sugar
is dissolved.
3. Fold in cream of
tartar, vanilla extract,
coconut and almonds.
Drop teaspoonfuls of the
mixture onto prepared
cookie sheets.
4. Bake for 30 minutes
or until crisp. Loosen
and allow to cool on
cookie sheets.

Coconut Almond Macaroons (top)
and Caramel Nut Tartlets.

Caramel Nut Tartlets

Preparation time:
  30 minutes
Total cooking time:
  30 minutes
Makes about 18

3/4 cup all-purpose
  flour
1 tablespoon sugar
1 1/4 oz butter
1 tablespoon milk

Filling
8 oz unsalted whole
  nut mix
1/2 cup sugar
1/4 cup water
1/4 cup cream

1. Preheat oven to
moderate 350°F. Sift
flour into a medium
mixing bowl; add sugar
and chopped butter.
Using fingertips, rub
butter into flour for
2 minutes or until
mixture is fine and
crumbly, stir in milk
and mix to a soft
dough. Turn onto
lightly floured surface,
knead for 1 minute or
until smooth.
2. Roll pastry thinly,
cut into circles using
a 2 1/2 inch fluted
round cutter. Press pastry
circles into greased
muffin top pans. Prick
evenly with a fork.

Bake for 10 minutes or
until lightly golden.
3. ***To make Filling:***
Spread nuts onto a
baking sheet. Bake for
10 minutes or until
lightly golden. Combine
sugar and water in a
medium pan. Stir
constantly over low
heat until sugar has
dissolved. Bring to boil.
Reduce heat, simmer
uncovered, without
stirring, for 10 minutes
or until golden brown.
Remove from heat, add
cream, stir until
combined. (If the syrup
sets in lumps when the
cream is added, return
pan to the heat for
1 minute or until
mixture becomes
smooth.) Add nuts,
stir until combined.
4. Spoon hot filling into
pastry shells, allow to
cool before serving.

HINT
The sugar and water
syrup should be a
medium golden
color when cooked.
If it is too pale, the
filling will not set. If
it becomes too dark,
it will burn. Cook
syrup over a low
heat. Remove pan
during the cooking
process to check if
the syrup is ready.

Cinnamon Fritters

Preparation time:
  10 minutes
Total cooking time:
  3 minutes per batch
Makes about 24

1 cup water
2 oz butter
2 tablespoons sugar
1 cup self-rising flour
4 eggs
oil for deep-frying
2 tablespoons
  confectioners'
  sugar
1 teaspoon ground
  cinnamon

1. Combine water, butter and sugar in a medium pan. Stir over low heat for 1 minute or until butter has melted; do not boil.
2. Remove pan from heat, add flour all at once. Using a wooden spoon, beat until smooth. Return to stove, heat until mixture thickens and comes away from side and base of pan. Remove from heat; cool slightly.
3. Transfer mixture to large mixing bowl. Using electric beaters, add eggs gradually, beating until mixture is glossy and thick.
4. Heat oil in a deep heavy-based pan over medium heat. Gently lower level tablespoons of mixture into oil in small batches. Cook over medium heat for 3 minutes or until golden brown and puffed. Carefully remove from oil with a slotted spoon. Drain on paper towel. Repeat with remaining mixture.
5. Place fritters on serving plate, dust with combined confectioners' sugar and cinnamon. Serve immediately.

Cheese and Pear Danish

Preparation time:
  20 minutes
Total cooking time:
  23 minutes
Makes 8

14 oz can pear halves
  in natural juice
8 oz cream cheese,
  softened
2 tablespoons sugar
1 teaspoon cornstarch
1 egg
2 teaspoons vanilla
  extract
2 sheets ready-made
  puff pastry
2 tablespoons sugar
1 tablespoon
  gelatin

1. Preheat oven to hot 475°F. Line two 13 x 11 inch baking sheets with waxed paper. Drain pears well; reserve one-third cup juice for glaze. Cut each pear half into thin slices.
2. Place cheese, sugar, cornstarch, egg and vanilla into small mixing bowl. Using electric beaters, beat on medium speed for 3 minutes or until mixture is creamy and smooth.
3. Cut each pastry sheet evenly into four squares. Place two heaped tablespoons cheese mixture diagonally across center of each pastry square. Overlap about three slices of pear onto cheese mixture at each end.
4. Carefully fold opposite ends of pastry over to enclose cheese filling; press to seal. Place on prepared baking sheets. Bake 20 minutes or until well puffed and lightly browned. Remove from oven, transfer to wire rack to cool.
5. Combine reserved pear juice, sugar and gelatin in small pan. Stir over low heat for 3 minutes or until sugar dissolves and mixture boils. Remove from heat; cool slightly. Brush cooled danish liberally with glaze. Allow glaze to set before serving.

*Cinnamon Fritters (top)
and Cheese and Pear Danish.*

Nut and Meringue Fingers

Preparation time:
  40 minutes
Total cooking time:
  30–35 minutes
Makes 16 pieces

4 oz butter
$^1/2$ cup sugar
1 egg
$1^1/2$ cups self-rising
  flour

Topping
$^1/2$ cup apricot jam
3 egg whites
$^1/2$ cup sugar
$^1/2$ cup (2 oz) finely
  chopped pecans
$^1/3$ cup (2 oz) finely
  chopped almonds

1. Preheat oven to moderate 350°F. Brush a shallow rectangular 12 x 8 inch cake pan with melted butter or oil. Line base and two sides with waxed paper.

2. Using electric beaters, beat butter and sugar in small mixing bowl until light and creamy. Add egg gradually, beating well.
3. Transfer mixture to large mixing bowl. Using a metal spoon fold in sifted flour, stir until just combined and the mixture is almost smooth. Spoon mixture evenly into prepared pan; smooth surface.

Prune, Apple and Almond Slice (left) and Nut and Meringue Fingers.

5. Bake for 35–40 minutes or until pastry is cooked and meringue set. Allow to cool before cutting into fingers.

Prune, Apple and Almond Slice

Preparation time:
 40 minutes
Total cooking time:
 1 hour
Makes 9 inch round

3¹/₂ oz unsalted butter
¹/₃ cup sugar
2 eggs
³/₄ cup all-purpose
 flour, sifted
12 oz smooth ricotta
 cheese
1 teaspoon grated lime
 rind
¹/₃ cup sugar, extra
2 eggs
¹/₃ cup chopped
 prunes
2 tablespoons
 cornstarch
13 oz can pie apple
1¹/₄ cups sliced
 almonds, toasted

1. Preheat oven to moderate 350°F. Brush a 9 inch round springform pan with melted butter or oil, line base with waxed paper; grease paper.
2. Using electric beaters, beat butter and sugar in small mixing bowl until light and creamy. Add eggs gradually, beating thoroughly after each addition. Add flour. Using a flat-bladed knife, mix to a thick paste. Spread/press mixture evenly over base of prepared pan. Bake for 20 minutes.
3. Place cheese, rind and sugar in small mixing bowl. Using electric beaters, beat until creamy. Add eggs gradually, beating thoroughly after each addition. Add prunes and cornstarch; beat until just combined. Transfer mixture to large mixing bowl.
4. Using a metal spoon, fold in the apple and half the almonds. Stir until just combined. Spoon mixture over pre-cooked base; smooth surface.
5. Scatter remaining almonds over cheese mixture; press gently onto surface. Bake for 55 minutes or until the filling is firm and golden. Cool in pan. To serve, cut into wedges. This slice is best stored in the refrigerator.

Note: You could substitute one-third cup fresh raspberries or blueberries for the prunes, if you prefer.

4. *To make Topping:* Spread pastry base evenly with jam. Place egg whites in small dry mixing bowl. Using electric beaters, beat egg whites until firm peaks form. Add sugar gradually, beating constantly until mixture is thick and glossy and all the sugar is dissolved. Carefully fold in nuts. Spread meringue mixture evenly over jam.

49

Honey Nut Strudel

Preparation time:
  40 minutes
Total cooking time:
  35 minutes
Serves 6–8

8 oz cream cheese,
  softened
2 egg yolks
2 tablespoons sugar
2 tablespoons honey
1/2 teaspoon ground
  cloves
2 1/2 cups chopped
  walnuts
1 cup ground almonds
3 oz butter, melted
10 sheets filo pastry

Honey Syrup
1/3 cup honey
2 tablespoons water
1 tablespoon lemon
  juice
1 teaspoon grated
  lemon rind
5 whole cloves

1. Preheat oven to
moderately hot 415°F.
Brush a deep, 8 inch
round springform pan
with melted butter or
oil, line base with
waxed paper; grease
paper. Place cheese,
yolks, sugar and honey
into small mixing bowl.
Using electric beaters,
beat 3 minutes on high
speed until light and
creamy. Add cloves
and nuts; stir with a
metal spoon until
just combined.

2. Place five sheets of
pastry onto work
surface. Keep remaining
sheets covered with a
damp cloth to prevent
sheets drying out. Brush
each sheet of pastry all
over with butter. Top
with second sheet of
pastry. Repeat process
until five sheets have
been layered. Do not
brush top sheet with
butter. Cover and set
aside. Repeat process
with remaining five
sheets of pastry.
3. Lay the two lots
of pastry lengthways
across work surface.
Brush along narrow
end of one lot of pastry
with butter. Carefully
overlap second lot of
pastry about 4 inches
onto buttered end.
(Pastry should now be
about 24 inches long.)
4. Spoon creamy nut
mixture evenly along
edge of pastry closest
to you, leaving a
4 inch border at each
end. Roll pastry over
to enclose filling. Fold
ends over to seal in
filling. Complete
rolling to end of pastry.
Brush all over with
remaining butter.
5. Beginning at one
end, carefully roll
the pastry into a
spiral, large enough
to fit the pan. Place into
prepared pan, bake
30 minutes or until
well browned and
crisp. Pour cooled

syrup over hot roll.
Cool in pan.
**6. *To make Honey
Syrup:*** Combine all
ingredients in small
pan. Stir over low heat
until mixture boils.
Simmer, uncovered,
without stirring, for
5 minutes.

Apricot Coconut Crescents

Preparation time:
  40 minutes
Total cooking time:
  50 minutes
Makes 16

1 1/2 cups chopped
  dried apricots
3/4 cup water
1 tablespoon butter
1/2 cup condensed
  milk
1/2 cup shredded
  coconut
1/2 teaspoon grated
  lime rind
4 sheets ready-made
  pie dough
1 egg white, lightly
  beaten
1/4 cup shredded
  coconut, extra

1. Preheat oven to
moderate 350°F. Line
a 13 x 11 inch baking
sheet with waxed paper.
Place the apricots,
water and butter in
small pan. Stir over
medium heat 3 minutes
or until mixture boils.
Reduce heat, simmer

Honey Nut Strudel (left) and Apricot Coconut Crescents.

uncovered, 12 minutes or until mixture is thick and almost all liquid is absorbed.

2. Add the milk, stir over low heat for 5 minutes. Remove from heat, add coconut and rind. Stir to combine; cool. Cut each pastry sheet evenly into four squares. Spread 1 tablespoon of mixture over a square, leaving one corner uncovered.

3. Roll opposite corner towards the uncovered corner of pastry, shape into a crescent. Repeat process with remaining pastry and filling.

4. Arrange crescents onto prepared baking sheet about 1¹/4 inches apart; brush with egg white. Sprinkle crescents with coconut. Bake for 25 minutes or until golden and cooked through. Leave on baking sheet 5 minutes before transferring to wire rack.

51

Savory

These scrumptious savories will do double duty—they're perfect at afternoon tea time, and will be equally at home with cocktails or pre-dinner drinks, as a first course for a dinner party or, served with a green salad, as a light lunch.

Sandwiches

Preparation time:
 35 minutes
Total cooking time:
 Nil
Serves 4–6

PINWHEEL SANDWICHES
1 loaf unsliced brown or
 white bread

Filling
*8 oz cream cheese,
 softened*
*1/2 cup finely chopped
 dates*
*3/4 cup finely chopped
 walnuts*
*1 teaspoon finely grated
 orange rind*

1. Cut crusts from loaf. Cut loaf lengthways into slices.
2. Combine cheese, dates, walnuts and orange rind.
3. Spread filling evenly onto each slice; roll up from either long or short side of bread. Wrap tightly in plastic wrap and refrigerate for 1 hour.
4. Slice into circles using a serrated knife.

FINGER SANDWICHES
*1/2 loaf white sliced
 bread*
*1 loaf whole wheat
 bread*
*8 oz unsalted butter,
 softened*

Filling 1
*8 oz can red salmon,
 drained, skin and
 bones removed*
*1 tablespoon
 mayonnaise*
*1 teaspoon lemon
 juice*
*1/2 teaspoon freshly
 ground black pepper*

Filling 2
*2 cucumbers, peeled and
 thinly sliced*
*1 teaspoon finely grated
 lemon rind*

*Pinwheel and Finger Sandwiches and Chive and
Onion Scones with Bacon Butter (page 54).*

1. Butter the white bread on both sides, whole wheat bread on one side only.
2. Combine salmon, mayonnaise, juice and pepper.
3. Place half of the whole wheat bread slices on a large flat surface. Spread evenly with salmon mixture. Top with white slices. Top with cucumber and lemon rind and finish with remaining whole wheat slices.
4. Using a serrated knife, remove crusts from sandwiches. Cut each sandwich into three fingers.

Note: Sandwiches are best made close to serving time. If necessary, they can be covered with plastic wrap and stored in the refrigerator for up to two hours.

Chive and Onion Scones with Bacon Butter

Preparation time:
  12 minutes
Total cooking time:
  25 minutes
Makes 32 pieces

Bacon Butter
3 oz butter, softened
2 teaspoons bacon
  bits

Chive and Onion Scones
3 cups self-rising flour
1 1/4 oz French onion
  soup mix
2 oz butter
1 cup milk
1 egg yolk
2 tablespoons freshly
  chopped chives
2 tablespoons milk, extra

1. Preheat oven to hot 475°F. Line a 13 x 11 inch baking sheet with waxed paper.
To make Bacon Butter: Combine butter and bacon bits in small bowl; mix well. Store, covered with plastic wrap, in refrigerator, 30 minutes.
2. Place flour, soup mix and butter in food processor bowl. Using the pulse action, press button for 15 seconds. Add milk, yolk and chives to bowl, process 5 seconds or until mixture almost forms a dough.
3. Turn dough onto lightly floured surface; knead for 30 seconds. Press mixture evenly into a floured shallow 12 x 8 inch rectangular pan. Turn out onto a floured board. Using a sharp knife, cut dough into 32 pieces. Brush

tops with extra milk.
4. Arrange pieces evenly apart onto prepared baking sheet. Bake for 10 minutes. Reduce temperature to moderately hot 415°F, and bake a further 15 minutes or until well risen and browned. Serve warm with chilled bacon butter.

Ham and Cheese Corn Bread

Preparation time:
  25 minutes
Total cooking time:
  30 minutes
Makes 16 pieces

1 cup self-rising flour
1 cup cornmeal
1 cup grated Cheddar
  cheese
3 thin slices (3 1/2 oz)
  ham, chopped
1/3 cup finely chopped
  parsley
1 cup milk
1/4 cup olive oil
2 eggs

1. Preheat oven to moderate 350°F. Brush a 12 x 8 inch shallow rectangular cake pan with melted butter or oil. Line base and sides with waxed paper; grease paper.
2. Sift flour into bowl. Add cornmeal, cheese, ham and parsley. Make a well in center.
3. Add combined milk,

Ham and Cheese Corn Bread.

olive oil and eggs to dry ingredients. Stir with wooden spoon until just combined; do not overbeat.
4. Pour mixture into prepared pan; smooth surface. Bake 30 minutes or until skewer comes out clean when inserted into center of corn bread. Stand bread in pan for 3 minutes before turning out onto a wire rack to cool.

Note: Yellow cornmeal is also known as polenta. It is available in fine, medium or coarse grind. Corn bread is best eaten on the day it is baked.

55

Choux Puffs with Savory Fillings

Preparation time:
1 hour 15 minutes
Total cooking time:
30 minutes
Makes 16 puffs

2 oz butter
³/4 cup water
³/4 cup all-purpose
   flour
3 eggs, beaten

Salmon Filling
2 oz butter
¹/4 cup all-purpose flour
1¹/4 cups milk
4 oz can red salmon,
   drained, skin and
   bones removed
2 teaspoons lemon juice
1 tablespoon mayonnaise
¹/3 cup finely chopped
   chives

Cheese Filling
³/4 oz butter
4 oz button
   mushrooms, thinly
   sliced

2 oz butter
¹/4 cup all-purpose flour
1 teaspoon freshly
   ground black pepper
1 cup milk
¹/4 cup cream
¹/2 cup grated Cheddar
   cheese
¹/4 cup finely chopped
   parsley

1. Preheat oven to moderately hot 415°F. Brush a 13 x 11 inch baking sheet with melted butter. Combine butter and water in medium pan. Stir over low heat until butter has melted; bring to boil.
2. Remove pan from heat, add flour all at once. Beat until smooth using a wooden spoon. Return to stove, heat until mixture thickens and comes away from side of pan. Remove from heat, cool slightly. Transfer mixture to large mixer bowl. Add eggs gradually, beating until mixture

is glossy and thick.
3. Spoon heaped tablespoons of pastry onto prepared baking sheets. Sprinkle with cold water. Bake 15 minutes. Reduce heat to moderate 350°F, bake further 15 minutes or until crisp and browned.
4. Cut puffs in half, remove any uncooked mixture. Return puffs to oven for 3–4 minutes or until dry. Spoon filling into base of each puff, replace tops and serve immediately.
5. *To make Salmon Filling:* Heat butter in medium pan; add flour. Stir over low heat 2 minutes or until flour mixture is lightly golden. Add milk gradually to pan, stirring until mixture is smooth. Stir continuously until mixture boils and thickens; boil further 1 minute; remove from heat. Stir in flaked salmon, lemon juice,

Stir flour mixture until it thickens and comes away from sides of pan.

Sprinkle heaped tablespoons of pastry with cold water.

Choux Puffs with Savory Fillings.

mayonnaise and chives; stir gently to combine.
6. *To make Cheese Filling:* Heat butter in medium pan, add mushrooms. Cook over low heat for 3 minutes or until mushrooms are just tender; add flour and pepper. Stir over low heat for 2 minutes or until flour mixture is lightly golden. Add combined milk and cream gradually to pan, stirring until the mixture is smooth. Stir continuously until the mixture boils and thickens; boil for a further 1 minute; remove from heat. Stir in cheese and parsley.

Cut puffs in half and remove any uncooked mixture from center.

For Salmon Filling, stir salmon, juice, mayonnaise and chives into flour mixture.

Individual Pumpkin Quiches

Preparation time:
  25 minutes + 15
  minutes refrigeration
Total cooking time:
  45 minutes
*Makes six 5 inch
quiches*

1¹/2 cups all-purpose
  flour
3 oz butter
2–3 tablespoons iced
  water

Filling
2 teaspoons oil
2 slices bacon, finely
  chopped
1 leek, sliced
3 eggs, lightly beaten
¹/2 cup cream
³/4 cup cooked,
  mashed pumpkin
  (8 oz raw)
³/4 cup grated Cheddar
  cheese

1. Preheat oven to
moderately hot 415°F.
Sift flour into a large
mixing bowl; add
chopped butter.
Using fingertips, rub
butter into flour for
2 minutes or until
mixture is fine and
crumbly. Add water,
mix to a soft dough.
Turn onto lightly
floured surface, knead
1 minute or until smooth.
Store, covered in plastic
wrap, in refrigerator
for 15 minutes.

2. Roll pastry between
two sheets of plastic
wrap, large enough to
cover six 5 inch quiche
pans. Cut a sheet of
waxed paper large
enough to cover pastry-
lined pan. Spread a layer
of dried beans or rice
evenly over paper. Bake
for 10 minutes. Remove
from oven; discard paper
and beans. Return pastry
to oven for 5 minutes
or until lightly golden.
3. *To make Filling:*
Combine oil, bacon and
leek in a medium pan,
stir over medium heat
for 5 minutes or until
lightly browned, cool.
4. Combine eggs and
cream in a large mixing
bowl, whisk until
just combined. Add
pumpkin, bacon
mixture and cheese,
stir until combined.
5. Pour filling into pastry
shells. Reduce the heat
to moderate 350°F. Bake
for 25 minutes or until
filling is lightly golden
and just set.

Note: Quiches can be
served warm or at room
temperature. Cut in
half for finger food or
leave whole for lunch.

Asparagus Frittata Fingers

Preparation time:
  20 minutes
Total cooking time:
  30 minutes
Makes about 20 fingers

¹/2 cup self-rising flour
6 eggs, lightly beaten
¹/2 cup oil
2 medium (6¹/2 oz)
  zucchini, grated
3 green onions, finely
  chopped
1¹/2 cups grated
  Cheddar cheese
11 oz can asparagus
  spears, drained

1. Preheat oven to
moderate 350°F. Brush
two 10¹/2 x 3 x 1³/4 inch
loaf pans with oil, line
base and sides with
waxed paper; grease
paper. Sift flour into
bowl, make a well in
the center. Add eggs
and oil, whisk until
just combined.
2. Add zucchini, green
onions and cheese, stir
until combined.
3. Spoon mixture evenly
into pans. Lay asparagus
spears diagonally over
mixture. Bake 30 minutes
or until lightly golden.
Turn out of pans, remove
paper, cut into diagonal
fingers. Serve warm or
at room temperature.

---

*Individual Pumpkin Quiches (top)
and Asparagus Frittata Fingers.*

Chili, Garlic and Parmesan Crescents

Preparation time:
  10 minutes + 30
  minutes refrigeration
Total cooking time:
  20 minutes
Makes 80

1¹/3 *cups all-purpose*
  flour
3¹/2 *oz grated Parmesan*
  cheese (1¹/4 cups)
pinch chili powder
¹/4 *teaspoon garlic salt*
3¹/2 *oz butter, chopped*
2 *egg yolks*
chili powder, extra
garlic salt, extra

1. Preheat oven to
moderately hot 415°F.
Line two 13 x 11 inch
baking sheets with
waxed paper.
2. Place flour, cheese,
chili, salt and butter in
food processor bowl.
Using the pulse action,
press button for
15 seconds. Add egg
yolks. Press button for
10 seconds or until
mixture forms a dough.
3. Turn onto a lightly
floured surface and shape
into an 8 inch long log.
Cover with plastic
wrap and refrigerate
for 30 minutes.
4. Cut the log into

¹/4 inch-thick rounds.
Cut each round in half.
Arrange on prepared
baking sheets ¹/4 inch
apart. Sprinkle lightly
with extra chili powder
and extra garlic salt.
5. Bake 20 minutes or
until lightly browned
and crisp. Transfer to
wire rack to cool.

Grand Marnier Pâté

Preparation time:
  15 minutes + 6 hours
  refrigeration
Total cooking time:
  10 minutes
Serves 8

3¹/2 *oz butter*
1 *lb chicken livers*
1 *medium onion,*
  chopped
1 *clove garlic, crushed*
¹/3 *cup Grand Marnier*
¹/3 *cup cream*
¹/2 *teaspoon dried sage*
¹/2 *teaspoon dried*
  thyme

1. Heat butter in a
large heavy-based
pan. Add livers, onion,
garlic and Grand
Marnier. Stir over a

medium heat until
livers are almost
cooked and onion is
soft. Bring to the boil,
simmer 5 minutes.
Remove from heat
and cool slightly.
2. Place mixture in
food processor bowl.
Using pulse action,
press button for
30 seconds or until
mixture is smooth.
Add cream and herbs,
process for a further
15 seconds.
3. Pour mixture into
a 3-cup capacity
ramekin, cover with
plastic wrap and
refrigerate for
6 hours, until firm.
Serve with melba
toast or crackers.

> HINT
> You can buy melba
> toast at
> supermarkets. To
> make your own,
> remove the crusts
> from slices of fresh
> bread. Flatten with
> a rolling pin and cut
> into desired shapes.
> Dry bread in 415°F
> oven for 10 minutes.
> Alternatively, toast
> white sandwich
> bread on both sides,
> remove crusts and
> slice through the
> center with a serrated
> knife, so that each
> slice is very thin and
> toasted on one side
> only. Toast the other
> side lightly.

Grand Marnier Pâté (top) and
Chili, Garlic and Parmesan Crescents.

Spicy Sausage Pinwheels

Preparation time:
  15 minutes
Total cooking time:
  20 minutes
Makes 25

4 oz sausage meat
1 small carrot, finely
  grated
1 green onion, finely
  chopped
1 clove garlic,
  crushed
2 teaspoons tomato
  paste
1 teaspoon curry
  powder
1 teaspoon chopped
  fresh rosemary
1 sheet ready-made
  puff pastry

1. Preheat oven to moderately hot 415°F. Line two 13 x 11 inch baking sheets with waxed paper. Combine sausage meat in a medium bowl with carrot, green onion, garlic, tomato paste, curry and rosemary.
2. Spread mixture evenly over pastry sheet and roll up to form a log. Using a sharp knife, cut log into 1/2 inch slices.
3. Lay slices about 1 1/2 inches apart on prepared baking sheets. Bake for 20 minutes or until lightly golden.

Note: Pinwheels are best eaten the day they are made, but can be kept in the refrigerator in an airtight container for up to two days. Reheat in a moderate oven for about 15 minutes before serving. Pinwheels can be frozen, cooked or uncooked, for three months. Freeze them on baking sheets before transferring them to a freezer bag, to ensure the pinwheels stay separated. Pinwheels are delicious served with tomato sauce for dipping.

Cheese Filo Slice

Preparation time:
  20 minutes
Total cooking time:
  25 minutes
Makes 20 pieces

8 oz ricotta cheese,
  mashed
6 1/2 oz feta cheese,
  crumbled
1 cup grated Cheddar
  cheese
1 egg, lightly beaten
pepper
1 tablespoon chopped
  fresh parsley
1/3 cup milk
1 tablespoon self-rising
  flour
1/4 cup olive oil
10 sheets filo pastry

1. Preheat oven to moderately hot 415°F. Brush a 12 x 8 inch shallow rectangular cake pan with oil. Combine the three cheeses, egg, pepper, parsley, milk and flour in a large mixing bowl. Using a fork, beat until ingredients are well mixed.
2. Place five sheets of pastry onto work surface. Keep remaining sheets covered with plastic wrap followed by a damp cloth to prevent sheets drying out. Brush oil over half a sheet of filo; fold in half. Place the folded pastry over the base of the prepared pan. Brush top of filo with oil. Repeat oiling, folding and layering process with the five sheets of filo.
3. Spread cheese mixture over the filo base; smooth surface. Repeat oiling, folding and layering process with remaining five sheets of pastry; trim edges with a sharp knife if necessary. Mark the slice into 20 squares; do not cut through to the base of the slice. Brush top with remaining oil.
4. Bake 25 minutes or until well browned and crisp. Remove from oven; cool in pan. Use a serrated knife to cut the slice.

Cheese Filo Slice (top)
and Spicy Sausage Pinwheels.

Index